THE REMARKAI

OF

BENJAMIN ZEPHANIAH

The Comprehensive New Biography of the Great British
Poet and Writer, including early life, Health Issues, and
Final Days.

William Christian

TABLE OF CONTENT

Overview

Benjamin Zephaniah, a luminary in the realms of literature, poetry, and activism, recently bid farewell to the world, leaving behind a legacy that echoes his profound contributions. In this biography, we embark on a journey to delve into the life of a remarkable individual whose impact reverberates through the pages of his poetry and the corridors of social change. As we explore the intricate tapestry of his existence, we pay homage to the man whose words transcended time and continue to resonate even in his absence

Background and Early Life

Born and raised in the thriving Birmingham suburb of Handsworth and came from modest origins that influenced the direction of his life. Dyslexia was identified during his early years, which served as a challenge to overcome the complexities of language. Despite this obstacle, Zephaniah was always attracted to the expressive power of speech, drawing inspiration from the lyrical skill of Jamaican toasters and the rich tapestry of sound system culture.

Zephaniah's formative years are used as a canvas to express the themes of resiliency and inventiveness. Handsworth was raised in a multicultural and varied environment that deeply influenced his understanding of linguistic subtleties and laid the groundwork for his future as a poet and wordsmith.

Benjamin Zephaniah's significance

Reading through Benjamin Zephaniah's life story, it's clear that his importance goes well beyond the realm of literature. He will be remembered as a key figure in the growth of Black British culture and as a source of empowerment and representation for future generations. Zephaniah's journey exemplifies the transformational power of words, as he advocated for justice and challenged social conventions via poetry.

Zephaniah's importance is also seen in his unwavering devotion to moral values. He was a unique individual who never wavered in his beliefs, as shown by his 2003 rejection of an OBE. His adamant resistance to the relics of the empire and its ties to the slave trade was the basis for his sacrifice. As he put it, "I've been fighting against the empire all my life, fighting against slavery and colonialism all my life." This ethical stand further highlighted Zephaniah's commitment to utilizing his art as a force for good.

In Memoriam

Benjamin Zephaniah passed away recently, leaving a profound loss in the literary and activism worlds. Zephaniah's resignation was announced via a heartfelt message on his social media accounts, which also disclosed those eight weeks earlier, he had received a brain tumor diagnosis. The poet passed away in the company of his loved ones, even though he received prompt medical attention.

"We shared him with the world, and we know many will be shocked and saddened by this news," reads the statement posted on Zephaniah's Instagram account, expressing his profound impact on people. This statement is echoed by admirers, fellow artists, and people whose lives were touched by his work. A collection of pieces that will always strike a chord with the public consciousness has been left behind by the lyrical voice that stood up for the oppressed and questioned the status quo.

We can honor the depth of Benjamin Zephaniah's accomplishments and recognize the loss left by his absence as we consider his life in memoriam. With his demise, his words, both an inspiration and a catalyst for change, now have a new poignancy. This biography's in-memoriam section serves as a place to celebrate not just the artist but also the person who inspired the work—the one who lived, loved, and changed the world forever.

Roots and Influences

His life is a complex tapestry, with the influences and origins that created his creative identity telling an intriguing story. In this investigation, we examine the cultural and family underpinnings that shaped his path and disentangle the strands of early influences that shaped his creative voice.

Family

Benjamin Zephaniah was born and reared in Handsworth, Birmingham, a city rich in ethnic diversity. His upbringing and cultural background were fertile grounds for developing his creative soul. Zephaniah's family, who blended the sounds of the Caribbean with the throbbing rhythms of Birmingham, was a microcosm of the diaspora experience, having been born to parents of Caribbean origin.

Zephaniah's attention was piqued by the vibrant family life and the way traditions interacted. The cadence of patois created a rhythmic image of ancestral homelands, and tales were recounted in the kitchens of the Caribbean. Zephaniah's lyrical story opened with this family tapestry, giving his poetry a depth that spoke to the sense of being dispersed.

His deep-rooted Caribbean roots served as a source of inspiration. Zephaniah's poetry reflected his culture's lively festivities, folktales, and oral traditions. The origins of his creative identity—a fusion of British reality, Caribbean rhythms, and a profound comprehension of the nuances of identity—were planted in this family embrace.

CHAPTER ONE

Early Influences and Inspirations

A variety of sources influenced Zephaniah's formative years in addition to his family's heart. The young poet's inquisitiveness flourished at Handsworth because of its diverse cultures and voices. Zephaniah used the urban environment, with its plethora of tales and hardships, as a canvas for his poetry.

Examining Zephaniah's early influences requires considering the significance of his dyslexia diagnosis throughout his school years. Rather than being a barrier, this difficulty inspired his original viewpoint on language. His inability to comprehend written language drove him toward oral traditions and spoken language's rhythmic flow. Zephaniah's early experience with hardship served as the impetus for his unique approach, which would eventually establish him as a pioneer in the dub poetry genre.

Zephaniah's literary journey was significantly shaped by the lyrical virtuosity of sound system culture and the echoes of Jamaican toasters. The young poet was struck by the toasters' use of wordplay, rhythmic cadences, and socially aware themes in their poetry. It was a musical education that gave him a sense of the transformative power of words beyond just melody.

Zephaniah was shaped during these early years by a convergence of creative influences. The sounds of Handsworth's streets, the warmth of Caribbean kitchens, and the difficulties associated with dyslexia came together to shape a voice that would later reverberate in activism and writing.

The youthful Zephaniah was similarly enchanted by literature. Classic and modern poetry and writings accompanied him on his quest for self-awareness. His creative palette expanded due to these literary inspirations and his insatiable curiosity. Zephaniah assimilated the range of human expression, from Shakespeare to the revolutionary poems of the Beat Generation, and woven it into the fabric of his developing personality.

Zephaniah's early experiences were shaped by various factors, much like the city that raised him. They were the patois-infused stories of his family circle, the rhythmic rhythms of reggae, his dyslexic problems, and the literary journey that broadened his perspective. These inspirations came together to create the poet who would become a trailblazer in dub poetry, breaking barriers and igniting debates.

Benjamin Zephaniah's origins and inspirations reveal that he was not just a poet but also a byproduct of his upbringing, demonstrating the interaction between his background and the multitude of voices reverberating through his early years. A literary agent that would resonate far beyond the streets of Handsworth and touch hearts and minds worldwide would develop due to the convergence of varied influences and family affection.

The Poet Emerges

The Poet Emerges in Benjamin Zephaniah's life story tells the story of his deep self-discovery, creative investigation, and life-changing discoveries. This section explores the early poems that served as the beginning of his creative journey and the critical turning points that thrust him into the public eye and cemented his reputation as a pioneer in the field of poetry.

Early Poetry and Creative Journey

Zephaniah's poetry began in the crucible of his adolescence when the streets of Handsworth served as both inspiration and canvas. The rich cultural environment around him influenced him, and his early poems served as a vehicle to express the pleasures, challenges, and complexity of his and his community's experiences.

Zephaniah's early poetry is full of raw, unadulterated energy that conveys the genuineness of a poet attempting to navigate the complex issues of race, identity, and social injustices. His pen turned into a tool for reflection, a way to peel back the layers of his life and give voice to the hidden stories around him.

Combining spoken word and reggae beats, Dub poetry became one of Zephaniah's most distinctive early artistic expressions. Inspired by the Jamaican toasters who had enthralled him as a young man, he developed a unique style that broke through traditional poetry conventions. This combination of rhyme and music became a defining feature of his work, turning the spoken word into a powerful tool for social critique and uplifting the ordinary to the spectacular.

Zephaniah's early poems functioned as a call to action against social injustices and a means of personal catharsis. Handsworth's poetry mirrored the racial tensions and economic hardships often plaguing the city. His writings served as a bridge, bringing his community's collective experiences to the attention of a worldwide readership eager for stories that cut across boundaries.

Evolution characterizes a poet's creative path, and Zephaniah's is no different. His early poems served as a springboard for a body of work that would inspire, stimulate, and test him. His personal experiences combined with Caribbean rhythms and reggae beats to produce a unique and poignant literary blend.

Breakthrough Moments

Although the path of a poet is often marked by slow development, certain times stand out as revolutionary breakthroughs—situations in which the artist breaks out from the shadows and into the public eye. These breakthrough experiences were significant not just for Benjamin Zephaniah personally but also as indicators of a growing cultural revolution.

A significant turning point was the release of his first poetry book, "Pen Rhythm," in 1980. This was Zephaniah's formal debut in literature, the moment his poetry sprang from the pages and into the minds and hearts of readers. The poem "Pen Rhythm" demonstrates the poet's ability to fuse linguistic skills with deep social awareness. There had been a clarion sound announcing the entrance of a new literary voice that would forever change the face of modern poetry.

The release of Zephaniah's album "Rasta," a musical interpretation of his dub poetry, marked another turning point in his career. The amalgamation of reggae beats and socially conscious poems resonated with listeners beyond traditional poetry groups. Zephaniah was thrust into a world where his lyrics could be heard on the radio and paper, connecting with a wide range of listeners and establishing him as a major figure in culture once "Rasta" was released.

 The innovations extended beyond the fields of music and literature. Zephaniah's entry onto mainstream radio, with performances on renowned stations like BBC Radio 4, helped to increase his notoriety. His lyrical interpretation of social themes reached a wider audience, slipping beyond the specialized borders of poetry enthusiasts and into the general public's awareness.

Without question, Zephaniah's 1987 appointment as a poet-in-residence in the Houses of Parliament in London was one of his most meaningful breakthroughs. This extraordinary action established him as a lyrical voice with the ability to impact political debate, symbolizing the acknowledgement of his creative excellence. It was evidence of the transforming power of language and the ability of poetry to worm its way into the most prestigious political circles.

Zephaniah's remarks gained power as his star rose higher and higher. With each new development, he dispelled earlier beliefs about the popularity and impact of poetry. His poems turned into hymns to change, striking a chord with readers everywhere and encouraging a new generation of poets to push the limits of the genre.

By examining the times when Zephaniah came out of hiding, we can see the artistic triumphs of the individual and the societal impact of a poet whose voice catalyzed social change. These innovations—whether in the lyrics of an album, on the pages of a book of poetry, or in the corridors of political authority—capsulate the spirit of a poet who broke free from tradition and made a lasting impression on the canvases of modern literature.

CHAPTER TWO

Activism and Advocacy

The chapters on activism and advocacy in Benjamin Zephaniah's complex character serve as a monument to the ability of words to effect social change and serve as creative expression. This investigation explores the depths of his involvement with political and social concerns, the relevance of his influence on current affairs, and the deft way activism is woven into the fabric of his literary creations.

Social and Political Activism

Zephaniah's entry into political and social engagement was a logical progression of the philosophy ingrained in his poems. His words echoed with the pulse of social injustices on the streets, not merely on the pages of books or in the rhythm of spoken poetry. His unrepentant activism, which included forcefully confronting the current quo, questioning social conventions, and standing hard against injustice, was one of its distinguishing features.

An important turning point in Zephaniah's activism journey came when he turned down an Order of the British Empire (OBE) in 2003. This act of conscientious opposition was a strong protest against the British Empire's historical links to colonialism and the slave trade, not just a rejection of a personal award. He clarified his position in an interview by stating, "I've been fighting against Empire all my life, fighting against slavery and colonialism all my life. So how could I accept an honor that puts the word Empire on my name? That would be hypocritical."

With this principled refusal, Zephaniah demonstrated his dedication to utilizing his platform for purposes beyond self-promotion. It struck a chord as a powerful proclamation that his loyalty was to the people and the quest for justice rather than to organizations connected to past wrongdoings.

Zephaniah was not content to stop at symbolic actions. He started speaking out in favour of issues like animal rights, anti-racism, and racial equality. His involvement with these concerns extended beyond his public remarks; he participated in demonstrations and supported the grassroots movements aiming for real change. By doing this, he personified the symbiotic link between art and activism, in which the artist catalyzes social change.

Zephaniah's Impact on Contemporary Issues

Zephaniah's advocacy has a considerably wider impact than his public statements and personal choices. It infuses the central theme of his poetry, in which he tackles modern problems with moral clarity and a keen understanding that echoes throughout the rhymes.

His poetry interweaves the themes of social injustice, racial prejudice, and the pursuit of justice into a cohesive whole. He tackles racial profiling and police violence in pieces like "Dis

Policeman Keeps on Kicking Me to Death," bringing attention to the structural problems that continues. Zephaniah's remarks mirror the social evils that everyone needs to pay attention to and take action against.

His interactions with educational institutions are another way that his advocacy has an influence. Zephaniah has been a strong proponent of educational change, especially when tackling racial injustice and advancing inclusion. His actions in this area are consistent with his conviction that education can be a powerful weapon for transforming society and eliminating structural inequities.

Zephaniah's influence on modern concerns extends beyond the borders of his own Britain. His support of social justice, environmental sustainability, and human rights cuts beyond national borders and is reflected in the struggles of oppressed people all over the globe. He has amplified the seriousness of problems requiring collective awareness and action by becoming a worldwide advocate for change via his engagement with organizations and campaigns.

Literary Works

Activism and Zephaniah's literary works have a complex and mutually beneficial relationship. His poetry is a battleground where words are used as weapons against tyranny, injustice, and prejudice. Every stanza serves as a rallying cry, an encouragement to face hard realities and explore the nuances of the human condition.

In compositions like "City Psalms," Zephaniah explores poverty, injustice, and social divisions by delving into the urban environment. The poems take on the qualities of the concrete jungles where systemic problems appear, providing readers with a literary prism through which to see the intricacies of modern urban life.

Zephaniah's anthology "Too Black, Too Strong" is a prime example of the union of activism and literature; it addresses racial discrimination, celebrates Black identity, and challenges the existing power structures. The poems in this book are social reform manifestos as much as works of literature. They insist on being heard, absorbed, and taken seriously in addition to just being read.

Zephaniah's entry into the young adult literary genre is another example of how art and activism may coexist. His works, including "Face" and "Refugee Boy," tackle racism, immigration, and cultural identity. He creates an understanding that goes beyond fiction by allowing readers to identify with the hardships of underprivileged people via gripping storylines.

Zephaniah's literary works have had an incalculable influence on modern concerns. His statements serve as catalysts for critical debate, igniting discussions that extend beyond the pages of books and into the public domain. Zephaniah's writings become canvases for the hopes of a more fair and equal society, whether via the rhythm of spoken words or written words on a page.

We see a smooth transition between words and acts as we follow Zephaniah through his life's activity and literary expression. His literary works became tools of social change because of his dedication to justice and equality and the amplifying of the voices of the oppressed. Every piece of poetry turns into a call to action, and every book demonstrates the power of narrative to change lives.

CHAPTER THREE

Overview of Major Works

Benjamin Zephaniah has created a vast body of work that reflects the rhythms of cultural identity and the cadence of social awareness. We explore the deep themes that run through his main results and the unique stylistic aspects that define his literary legacy as we go through the hallways of his works.

Zephaniah's early works started his literary voyage, with the release of "Pen Rhythm" in 1980 being one of the first significant achievements. This book heralded his entry into the academic world, exposing readers to the objective, raw poetry that would later define his style. It was a debut that predicted the path of a poet fearless in the face of social injustice and negotiating the nuances of identity.

The song "Rasta, Far I" was an important turning point in Zephaniah's life since it united poetry with music. The album, released in 1982, demonstrated his trademark of fusing spoken word with reggae sounds, which would be associated with him. "Rasta, Far I" was more than simply a musical project; it was a declaration of culture, fusing Zephaniah's poetic skill with the rhythmic legacy of Jamaica to create a distinctive soundscape that impacted listeners far beyond the poetry genre.

Zephaniah's body of work broadened in scope as his literary repertory grew. The 1992 collection "City Psalms" explored the urban experience and provided moving commentary on poverty, injustice, and the rifts in modern society. This collection of poems acts as a literary microscope, illuminating the harsh realities of urban life while maintaining a thread of optimism that seeps into even the most desolate areas.

Zephaniah's "Too Black, Too Strong" (2001) unprecedentedly elevated his examination of social and political subjects. This collection fought institutional injustices, addressed racial prejudice, and embraced the Black identity. The poems in this book are not just works of literature; they are calls for social change that must be heard, understood, and responded to in addition to being read.

Within the fiction genre, Zephaniah's books have had a lasting impression. Racism, immigration, and cultural identity are topics covered in "Face" (1999) and "Refugee Boy" (2001). He creates an understanding that goes beyond fiction by allowing readers to identify with the hardships of underprivileged people via gripping storylines. Zephaniah's ability to easily move between poetry and prose and maintain his narrative voice across several literary genres is on display in these works.

Zephaniah's work in children's books demonstrates the diversity of his creative pursuits. His ability to engage young minds with issues of social justice, diversity, and the appreciation of cultural heritage is seen in the films "J is for

Jamaica" (2006) and "Wicked World!" (2000). these pieces highlight Zephaniah's dedication to using storytelling's transformational potential to mound the minds of the next generations.

Analysis of Style and Themes

Zephaniah's writing dynamically combines rhythmic energy, frank honesty, and vibrant language. Drawing on his Jamaican roots and the diverse population of Handsworth, his language usage is an ode to the variety seen in spoken word expression. His lines offer a unique audio experience that goes beyond the printed word, combining patois, reggae rhythms, and the throbbing cadence of spoken language.

Zephaniah's paintings cover a wide range of landscapes, and so do the ideas that underlie them. His poems' key themes include racial equality, social justice, cultural identity, and the complexities of urban living. With a keen sense of observation, he challenges social conventions and invites readers to grapple with the harsh reality of systematic injustices.

In-depth examinations of identity are among Zephaniah's poetry's recurrent subjects. Whether exploring his experiences as a Black man living in Britain or honoring the diversity of his cultural background, Zephaniah's poetry provides a window into the complexity of the human condition. His poetry is a declaration that cuts across racial and cultural barriers, affirming both individual and community identity.

Zephaniah paints his creative strokes on the socio-political scene. His poetry is an uncompromising reaction to social injustices, a kind of activism. Every poem becomes a rallying cry against injustice, prejudice, and the misuse of power, and they become instruments for overthrowing repressive structures. Zephaniah's dedication to justice is a fundamental part of his creative purpose and is not limited to the literary domain.

Zephaniah's origins in dub poetry, a form that combines spoken word with reggae rhythms, are evident in the rhythmic aspect of his poems. His lines' melodic quality turns poetry into a visceral experience that invites readers to experience the words' throbbing vitality in addition to their meaning. Because of this stylistic decision, he stands out in the literary world and gives his works a dynamic life.

Zephaniah's work is a means of social participation when one looks at his subjects and literary style. His poetry serves as a medium for discussions that go past literary boundaries and into the core of popular culture. His unwavering activity, cultural diversity, and linguistic agility define Zephaniah's academic signature.

Multifaceted Artistry

Zephaniah's inventiveness is diverse, which sets him apart as an artist. He moves fluidly between poetry and music, fiction and non-fiction, and adult and children's books. This adaptability reflects a creative mentality unconstrained by artistic traditions rather than just a show of technical proficiency.

Zephaniah has shown his capacity to go beyond the conventional bounds of poetic expression by publishing albums such as "Rasta, Far I" and incorporating reggae rhythms into his poems. His thoughts are not limited to the printed word; they also reverberate throughout radio and television, reaching listeners who may not otherwise be drawn to poetry. His artistic ability to use music broadens the audience to whom he can convey his message and welcomes them into his lyrical universe.

Zephaniah's venture into fiction is another example of his diverse artistic abilities. "Face" and "Refugee Boy" are not just books but narrative storytelling endeavors that carry his literary voice further. He expands upon the issues of racism, cultural identity, and the human experience that characterize his poetry in his novels. The breadth of his creative palette is shown by his ability to craft gripping stories while maintaining the core of his lyrical approach.

Zephaniah uses children's books as yet another medium for his artistic expression. Through books like "Wicked World!" and "J is for Jamaica," he teaches young readers important lessons about diversity, social justice, and ethnic pride. His dedication to using literature to mould young brains confirms his conviction that narrative can change people of all ages.

Zephaniah's artistic talent is wider than textual expression. His poetry comes to life via his immersive performances, available on recordings or stage. The spoken word takes on a life of its own and connects with the listener in a way written language cannot. Each reading becomes a fascinating voyage through his words' landscapes thanks to the performance element of his creativity.

When we consider Zephaniah's diverse artistic abilities, we see a creator unafraid of creative limitations. His ability to easily switch between several mediums illustrates a comprehensive view of art as a dynamic, living thing that changes along with the artist. Zephaniah's creative output is a kaleidoscope that entices viewers to interact with his pieces via various media and recognize the extent and profundity of his literary and other contributions.

CHAPTER FOUR

Beyond Poetry Music and Performance

Zephaniah is a poet whose creative path touches on performance, music, and poetry. This section highlights the synthesis of linguistic expression with musicality that characterizes his unique contribution to the world of artistic performance by examining the symbiotic link between his poetry lines and the rhythmic cadences of reggae.

Zephaniah's musical endeavours are a logical progression of his lyrical abilities. The publication of albums like "Belly of de Beast" (1996) and "Rasta, Far I" (1982) highlights his capacity to go beyond the limitations of spoken word and musical expression. His lyrics unfurl against reggae rhythms on these albums, resulting in a perfect synergy that enhances the listening experience.

In Zephaniah's writing, poetry and music are married, but not just any old sound is added; rather, they are carefully and intricately combined to maximize the effect of each. His spoken rhymes have a cadence complemented by the rhythmic pulse of reggae beats, which makes each piece seem vibrant and culturally vibrant. The musical element gives his remarks more depth and passion, enabling listeners to experience the throbbing energy of each performance with their ears and bodies.

His live performances enhance the dynamic interplay between music and words even further. Zephaniah commands attention with his captivating presence and skillfully weaves stories via spoken word, bringing melody to each lyric. The audience is drawn into the multisensory complexity of his performance as the stage is transformed into a platform for a whole creative experience where the lines between music and poetry are blurred.

Reggae, which originates in Jamaican social awareness and culture, has a strong complementing effect on Zephaniah's artistic themes. Spoken words combined with reggae beats are reminiscent of dub poetry, originating in Jamaican sound system culture that combined poetry with reggae rhythms. By following this custom, Zephaniah broadens the audience for his creative expression and respects the cultural legacy that moulded him—audiences enthralled by the enchantment of reggae music.

Zephaniah's live performances, in addition to his recorded albums, provide evidence of the powerful symbiosis between poetry and music. His ability to enthrall audiences with a blend of spoken word and reggae rhythms, whether on festival stages or in small settings, turns every performance into a celebration of language and musical creativity. Zephaniah breaks beyond the traditional limits of creative expression with its smooth integration, producing an immersive experience that leaves a lasting impression on all who see it.

Zephaniah's Contribution to the Arts

Beyond his work as a musician and poet, Benjamin Zephaniah has had a significant influence on the arts. This section explores the wider range of his achievements, which include activism, writing, and his impact on culture. Zephaniah's multifaceted involvement in the arts solidifies his status as a cultural provocateur, his impact going far beyond the written and spoken word.

1. Literary Contributions: Zephaniah has produced many literary works, including children's books, novels, and poetry. His socially oriented and vibrantly written poetry has become change-agent hymns. Works such as "Face" and "Refugee Boy" explore topics of immigration, racism, and cultural identity, demonstrating his skill at crafting engaging stories. Works in children's literature such as "J is for Jamaica" and "Wicked World!" show his dedication to forming young minds with tales that teach important lessons about diversity and social justice.

2. Activism and Social Commentary: Zephaniah's creative pursuits are inextricably linked to his activism. His 2003 rejection of an OBE and outspoken opposition to colonialism, slavery, and imperialism are prime examples of his moral dedication to social justice. He tackles difficult urban life in the modern day, police violence, and racial inequity in his

poems. Zephaniah is a living example of an artist who transforms creativity into practical activism because he actively works with grassroots movements and participates in rallies. His influence goes beyond the written word.

3. Initiatives in Education: Zephaniah's impact is seen in education, where he supports curriculum reform to remove racial prejudice and foster diversity. His involvement with academic institutions shows that he is dedicated to reshaping history and cultural identity narratives. He develops into more than simply a poet via talks, workshops, and outreach; he also catalyzes thought-provoking discussions in academic settings.

4. Broadcasting and Media: Zephaniah's impact reaches a broader audience because of his involvement in mainstream broadcasting, which includes appearances on stations like BBC Radio 4. His spoken word performances catch on with people who would not normally be interested in poetry over the airways. Zephaniah broadens the scope of the arts by dismantling barriers and extending an invitation to a wide range of listeners to engage with poetic expression.

5. Global Cultural Impact: Zephaniah has a significant worldwide impact, particularly in cultural representation and identity. Being a Black British artist, he fills a need that dispels myths and broadens the definition of being British. Due to his influence on the international scene, he is regarded as a cultural ambassador who promotes variety, inclusiveness, and the value of intercultural experiences.

Difficulties and Successes

Zephaniah's creative career has been characterized by setbacks as much as victories. This section delves into the challenges he encountered, the achievements he attained, and the tenacity that describes his lasting impact.

Difficulties

1. Dyslexia: **Although Zephaniah's early dyslexia diagnosis may have been seen as a barrier, he used it as inspiration for his distinct viewpoint on language. Dyslexia's obstacles led him to focus on oral traditions and the rhythmic flow of spoken language, which helped him develop the unique style that would come to be associated with his name.**

2. Systemic Injustices: **Zephaniah has sometimes defied accepted rules since his poetry confronts systemic injustices head-on without hesitation. His brave rejection of an OBE because of its ties to the British Empire is a prime example of his will to take on institutions that uphold the wrongs of the past.**

3. Social and Political Controversies: **Because of Zephaniah's vocal activity, there have been conflicts and disagreements with both social and political authorities. His determination to question the current quo has been met with backlash and hostility, whether he is declining accolades or bringing up delicate subjects.**

Achievements

1. Creative Acclaim: Zephaniah has received extensive recognition for his creative accomplishments, which include the release of well-received poetry collections and novels. His position as a well-known author of modern literature has been cemented by the critical accolades his work has garnered.

2. Cultural Impact: Zephaniah's influence on how Black British artists are seen in culture is a remarkable accomplishment in and of itself. His inhabiting of historically underrepresented locations has helped widen the narrative of cultural variety and reshape conceptions of identity.

3. Activism and Advocacy: Zephaniah's activism, whether expressed in his poems, remarks spoken in public, or involvement in social movements, is an example of how values win over recognition. His dedication to using his position for advocacy highlights the possibilities of Art as a catalyst for social transformation.

4. Global Reach: Zephaniah's impact as a poet and cultural icon has spread worldwide, signifying success in eradicating boundaries based on geography and culture. His remarks struck a chord with listeners everywhere, igniting a worldwide dialogue about justice, identity, and the human condition.

The difficulties and victories Benjamin Zephaniah encounters along the way are essential to the story of an artist who never wavers in his dedication to social justice, creative expression, and the transformational potential of language. Zephaniah succeeds in negotiating these tensions and comes out as a poet and a cultural figure whose influence goes beyond the confines of literature and into the hearts of those his work has impacted.

Personal Struggles

Personal hardships that have molded Zephaniah's personality and constituted a fundamental part of his creative expression have characterized his path. Being diagnosed with dyslexia during his school years was one of the major obstacles he had to overcome in his early life. This learning gap would have been seen as a hurdle in a culture that often values traditional academic accomplishments. Zephaniah, nevertheless, turned this obstacle into a chance.

Rather than impeding his connection with language, dyslexia was a driving force behind his distinctive use of language. Zephaniah discovered a voice by embracing spoken language and oral traditions, resonating beyond the limitations of conventional literary rules. Rather than confining him, this personal struggle inspired his unique approach, making him stand out in the spoken word and poetry communities.

Zephaniah's path is entwined with his experiences as a Black man in Britain in addition to his dyslexia. His creative themes were framed by the socio-political milieu of the day, which was characterized by systematic disparities and racial conflicts. His poetry evolved to address issues such as social injustice, racial prejudice, and the challenges of managing identity in a heterogeneous society. His poetry was filled with passion and intensity due to the personal problems he had due to these social issues, which turned his work into a vehicle for social criticism and change.

Professional Milestones

Zephaniah's career path is evidence of his adaptability and the breadth of his creative pursuits. The release of his poetry book "Pen Rhythm" in 1980, which heralded his entry into the literary scene, was one of his early achievements. With this first work, he demonstrated the unadulterated force of his words and laid the groundwork for a career navigating the intersections of activism, poetry, music, and fiction.

Zephaniah's poetry found a rhythmic counterpart in reggae music with the publication of the album "Rasta, Far I" in 1982, marking a pivotal moment in his creative development. This combination of spoken word and music expanded his creative expression beyond traditional poetry readings. The popularity of this record not only made him a recognized vocal word performer and strengthened his ties to the flourishing reggae culture.

Zephaniah's venture into fiction enhanced his career much more. He has shown in the books "Face" (1999) and "Refugee Boy" (2001) that he can write gripping stories that tackle important societal themes, including racism, immigration, and cultural identity. He reached a wider audience with fiction, speaking to those who weren't only poetry fans. His contributions to children's literature, such as "Wicked World!" (2000) and "J is for Jamaica" (2006), had a significant influence. Here, Zephaniah demonstrated his dedication to educating young people by using storytelling to teach diversity, social justice, and cultural heritage.

Zephaniah's professional path also included broadcasting, as seen by his performances on BBC Radio 4. He made his poems more widely available by using radio and other media, reaching readers who would have preferred to skip regular poetry readings. This range of venues demonstrates his versatility and his commitment to elevating poetry to the status of a vibrant and inclusive art form.

CHAPTER FIVE

Acknowledgment and Honors

The acknowledgement given to Benjamin Zephaniah is proof of his lasting impact on the literary and cultural scene. Honors and prizes are indications of an artist's influence on audiences and the larger cultural conversation, even if they are also external validation.

An important turning point in Zephaniah's history with awards and accolades was his 2003 rejection of an OBE. His stubborn refusal became a landmark act of resistance, as he pointed out how the Order of British Imperialism was linked to the historical history of slavery and imperialism. This refusal was a strong declaration of his ideals and his dedication to utilizing his position consistent with his beliefs rather than a rejection of recognition.

Zephaniah has won praise from various sources while turning down conventional awards. His poetry has received acclaim for its ability to cross traditional boundaries, social critique, and vibrant language. Peers and reviewers alike have come to admire him for the lasting influence of his work on modern literature.

Zephaniah is well known for his impact on how culture is portrayed, especially in light of his status as a Black British musician. As a cultural provocateur, he dispels myths and broadens the definition of being British. His influence on international conversations about diversity and identity is in and of itself an honor that goes beyond the conventional kind.

Zephaniah has won other honors that recognize his achievements, even if his rejection of a customary prize was a protest against the historical significance of such recognitions. He was among Britain's best 50 post-war novelists in The Times in 2008. Even if they weren't the main goal of his creative journey, these recognitions support the work's ongoing relevance and impact.

 Benjamin Zephaniah's path is a complicated story of perseverance, ingenuity, and unshakable determination as he navigates personal obstacles, achieves professional milestones, and gains acclaim. He is a cultural icon whose influence is felt in the written and spoken word and the transformative power of a life dedicated to art and activism. His refusal to conform to conventional expectations reflects his art and his stance on honours.

Recognition and Awards

Zephaniah has received several awards and distinctions over his lengthy career, celebrating his tremendous influence on poetry, literature, and cultural conversation. These honours, which range from prominent literary awards to recognition of his function as a cultural provocateur, bear witness to the continuing legacy of a creator who dared to push the limits of poetry and redefine norms.

Zephaniah's abiding disdain for awards is shown by his 2003 reluctance to accept an Order of the British Empire (OBE). His strong objection to the OBE's historical ties to slavery and imperialism led to this act of rebellion, which came to represent his dedication to social justice and sincerity. Zephaniah's denial sent shockwaves across the political and artistic domains since it was a strong declaration of his principles rather than a rejection of recognition.

Despite declining conventional rewards, Zephaniah has received recognition for his achievements in several ways. Affirming his status as one of literature's greats, The Times listed him among Britain's best 50 post-war authors in 2008. This appreciation reflected the widespread recognition and critical praise that his poetry had received over the years, a distinction that went beyond poetry to have wider cultural resonance.

One of Zephaniah's greatest achievements, apart from official recognition, is his influence on cultural representation. He expanded the narrative of cultural diversity and challenged preconceptions by occupying historically underrepresented locations for Black British artists. His impact on international conversations about identity and the value of intercultural experiences is recognition of his function as a cultural provocateur.

Zephaniah's poetry has won praise for its vivid language, social insight, and capacity to connect with a wide range of readers. His standing as a significant character in modern literature has been cemented by the recognition of critics, academics, and readers alike for the ongoing significance of his work.

Memorials Preserving Zephaniah's Everlasting Legacy

Posthumous tributes are painful reminders of the artist's legacy on the cultural environment, as with any artist whose influence transcends time. Even though Benjamin Zephaniah's literary and activist achievements will always be felt via his works, posthumous tributes serve as a way for people to show their appreciation for a life devoted to the arts and social change.

After his departure, the literary community lamented the loss of a visionary poet and cultural icon. Poets, activists, and fans flocked to pay their respects, realizing Zephaniah's lasting impact on social justice and poetry. For those who sought comfort and inspiration in his poetry, the force of his words— now preserved in writing and performance—persisted.

Zephaniah's writings are still being examined and valued in the scholarly community. Academics study his poetry in detail by exploring the relationships between language, identity, and social critique. Posthumous homages in educational settings help to sustain the discussion about his accomplishments, guaranteeing that his influence will always be a topic of interest and respect.

Institutions and groups dedicated to culture are also essential to maintaining Zephaniah's legacy. Events, retrospectives, and exhibitions devoted to his life and creations pay homage to him by introducing his art to new audiences and reinforcing his importance in the larger cultural fabric. These memorials serve as a means of remembering him and a chance to share his stirring stories with future generations.

Social media serves as a platform for collective memory in the digital era. Platforms are used by supporters, other artists, and activists to discuss their favorite poems of Zephaniah, consider the significance of his activity, and show thanks for the words' resonant influence on their lives. The internet becomes a virtual monument where people may still hear Zephaniah's voice via shared quotations, hash tags, and poignant notes.

Ultimately, Benjamin Zephaniah's posthumous honors acknowledge that his campaigning and artistic talent extended beyond his life on Earth. They turn into a never-ending celebration of a life devoted to justice, creativity, and the transformational potential of words. Every honor, official or unofficial, adds a stroke to the memorial canvas, painting a communal image of an artist whose influence transcends borders and generations and never stops inspiring, challenging, and resonating.

Chosen Interviews

Throughout his career, Benjamin Zephaniah—a poet with unmatched depth and cultural influence—has participated in several interviews. These discussions allow us a peek into his ideas, convictions, and complex self-concept. Here, we explore a few chosen conversations that provide special insights into this literary great's heart and intellect.

1. Zephaniah talks about his activism, poetry, and life in this BBC Hardtalk interview with Stephen Sackur. The discussion explores the connections between his life experiences, creative process, and unwavering dedication to social justice. Zephaniah's open answers provide insight into his reasons for declining an OBE, his opinions on current affairs, and the function of poetry in changing society.

2. The Big Narstie Show (2020) may be in demand atThe Big Narstie Show, a vibrant and casual environment, perfectly portrays Zephaniah's spirit as he converses with the presenters in a laid-back and hilarious manner. This conversation reveals a lighter side of the poet while retaining his signature wit and insight as it touches on subjects ranging from his early life to his thoughts on empire and colonialism.

3. Interview with Benjamin Zephaniah at Rolling Stones: A New Dawn, published in August Zephaniah considers his life and the development of his poems in this interview. The conversation includes his experiences with prejudice, how his dyslexia has affected his creative development, and how

music has greatly influenced how he writes poetry. Readers will have a greater understanding of the human events that Zephaniah used to inspire his potent and moving poetry via this discussion.

4. The 2019 "Can Words Change the World?"

Zephaniah's TEDx Talk is an engaging solo performance that defies convention by delving into the transforming power of words. He expresses his conviction that language can bring about significant transformation in spoken word poetry and autobiographical tales. This address summed up his opinions on the agency of words and their capacity to influence society's narratives.

Exploring His Essays, Speeches, and Reflections

Benjamin Zephaniah has written articles, lectures, observations, and interviews. Through his works, he can express his opinions on various topics, from deep insights into identity and action to the nuances of language.

1. The essay "The Future of Language" by Benjamin Zephaniah was published in 2015; Zephaniah considers how language has changed in the digital era in this insightful article. He talks about how technology affects communication and how it could affect speech variety. Zephaniah's investigation encourages readers to think about the dynamic interplay of language, culture, and advancement.

2. This is the 2019 Oxford Union Address

Zephaniah had the opportunity to talk about various subjects during his speech at the Oxford Union, including dyslexia, education, and the place of poets in society. His passionate and insightful speech highlights the value of diversity in education and encapsulates the spirit of his work. Zephaniah's words ring true as an appeal to question conventions and welcome inclusion.

3. The Guardian (2018) published a reflection titled "Why I Write"

In his reflections on his writing career, Zephaniah explains the inspirations for his work. He reveals the motivations that give his poetry its genuineness and resonance, ranging from the impact of reggae music to the potency of narrative. This contemplation offers insightful information on the inner workings of his creative mind.

Chronology of Significant Events

The life and career timeline of Benjamin Zephaniah is a story filled with significant events, sea change, and the development of his creative and activist persona. This timeline provides a chronological examination of important occasions that have influenced the course of this exceptional poet's life:

1. 1958 - April 15, at Handsworth, Birmingham, United Kingdom:

Benjamin Zephaniah was born in Handsworth, Pennsylvania, into a society that will provide the backdrop for his creative creations and social commentary.

2. 1970s: Dyslexia diagnosis:

Though at first difficult, Zephaniah's early experience with dyslexia turns into a transforming force that shapes his distinct approach to language.

3. The "Pen Rhythm" Poetry Collection was released in 1980.

With the publication of Zephaniah's first poetry book, "Pen Rhythm," a new voice in poetry is introduced.

4. The album "Rasta, Far I" was released in 1982.

The album "Rasta, Far I" has a pioneering moment when Zephaniah's spoken word is blended with reggae music, establishing him as a spoken word artist with a musical dimension.

5. 2003 - OBE Refusal:

Zephaniah declined to be an Order of British Colonialism (OBE) as a show of principled opposition, pointing out the organization's past ties to slavery and colonialism.

6. 2008-Listed among the top British companies in The Times

7. 50 Writers after the War:

Zephaniah's reputation as one of the most significant authors in post-war Britain is confirmed by his recognition from The Times.

8. 2019 - Address of Oxford Union:

Zephaniah uses his speech to the Oxford Union as a forum to discuss diversity, education, and the place of poets in society.

9. 2023 - Benjamin Zephaniah's Departure

A literary genius has passed away, yet his writings, advocacy, and influence on cultural narratives ensure that his legacy endures. His death is marked with sadness.

This timeline demonstrates the complexity of Benjamin Zephaniah's path, characterized by social activity, creative invention, and a dedication to questioning the existing quo. Every information in this timeline adds to the intricate picture of a life devoted to poetry, justice, and language.

Final Weeks and Passing: Reflecting on the Closing Chapter of a Literary Icon

A brain tumor diagnosis presented complications for Benjamin Zephaniah in the last weeks before his death. Zephaniah embodied resilience and stayed connected to the world and his work despite the seriousness of his physical situation.

Zephaniah's wife remained at his side throughout his sickness, and his family and close friends supported him during these last weeks. The world was shocked to learn of his death, as admirers, fellow artists, and fans struggled to come to terms with the loss of a cultural giant.

Zephaniah's death ended a life devoted to poetry, activism, and questioning social conventions. The global outpouring of grief and tributes demonstrated his deep influence on people and communities. His legacy endured beyond death because of the lasting impact of his activity and the words he left behind after his passing.

A Few Poems and Excerpts

The poetry of Benjamin Zephaniah is a tapestry woven with words that speak to social awareness, linguistic vitality, and a strong sense of place. Here are a few poems and passages that best express his creative genius:

1. Dis Poetry

Excerpt: "Dis poetry is not afraid of going in bookshop / a coolie-man shop / It's not afraid of going ina rich folks place / it's not afraid of going ina poor folks space."

2. To Do With Me

Excerpt: "So mi tek me suitcase a mi move to Wolverhampton / Mi haffi do dis caw mi love mi nation / But when mi reaches Wolverhampton mi heart turn heavy / Dem say mi accent was too heavy." *

3. Talking about Turkeys

Excerpt: "Be nice to you turkey dis Christmas / Cos' turkeys just wanna have fun / Turkeys are cool, turkeys are wicked / An every turkey has a Mum." *

4. Hurricane Blues

Excerpt: "But the hurricane is no gentleman the hurricane is no man / The hurricane is a lady / So I'm going back to find my man."

These chosen poems and fragments show the many subjects and literary forms that characterized Zephaniah's poetry. Through his whimsical use of language and his sensitive observations on identity and societal challenges, his words have left an enduring impression on those affected by his work and continue reverberating through the literary canon.

CONCLUSION

The last notes of Benjamin Zephaniah's life do not signal his demise but rather his legacy, which endures in the hearts of those impacted by his activism, teachings, and unwavering spirit. Literary great and cultural icon Zephaniah broke the rules, questioned accepted wisdom, and used ink that pulsed with the rhythms of his experiences to inscribe his story onto the canvases of British literature.

From his 1958 birth in Handsworth, Birmingham, to the closing chapters of his life characterized by the news of a brain tumour, Zephaniah's voyage took him across social and linguistic landscapes. Rather than being a barrier, his dyslexia diagnosis in the 1970s served as the impetus for a special bond with language and the creation of poetry that had an impact beyond traditional verse's parameters.

His official literary debut was "Pen Rhythm" in 1980. Then, in 1982, he released the "Rasta, Far I" album, which signified a symbiotic union of spoken word and reggae and cemented his reputation as a trailblazer in synthesizing poetry and music. In 2003, Zephyr

Zephaniah's placement in The Times' 2008 list of Britain's best 50 post-war authors confirmed his status as one of the country's leading writers after his uncompromising stance. His varied career included poetry books, novels, children's books, and music, demonstrating a creative adaptability that was impossible to pin down.

Zephaniah's influence may be seen in activism, cultural representation, and artistic endeavors. His poetry developed into a powerful medium for discussing racial conflicts, social difficulties, and the complexities of identity in a multicultural setting. His constant campaign for a more equal society and his unwillingness to accept accolades associated with past atrocities demonstrated his unshakeable dedication to social justice, which extended beyond words on a page.

Zephaniah exhibited a remarkable fortitude in the face of sickness during the last few weeks of his life. He continued living according to the spirit of his poems, surrounded by his family's support, overcoming obstacles with a fortitude derived from life experience. Upon learning of his death in 2023, fans worldwide showered him with tributes, each attesting to the poet's ongoing influence as an advocate of inclusion, a cultural provocateur, and a voice for the voiceless.

Snippets and a few chosen poems provide insights into Zephaniah's creative genius. From the upbeat rhythm of "Dis Poetry" to the moving introspection of "Hurricane Blues," his words never die and entice readers to explore his created mental and emotional worlds. These passages are dynamic, living things that inspire new generations and create a link over time and distance.

Conclusively, the legacy of Benjamin Zephaniah extends an invitation to delve into the subtleties of language, challenge social inequities, and acknowledge the transforming potential of words. His voyage, with its nuances, difficulties, and victories, makes a lasting impression on literature and popular culture. When we consider the life of this great poet, we are reminded that his influence endures beyond the pages of a biography—in the hearts of people who find comfort, motivation, and a call to action in Benjamin Zephaniah's poetry.

Printed in Great Britain
by Amazon

39687921R00030